Veterans Day

Maria Koran

Go to **www.eyediscover.com** and enter this book's unique code.

BOOK CODE

AVL68349

EYEDISCOVER brings you optic readalongs that support active learning.

Published by AV2
14 Penn Plaza 9th Floor
New York, NY 10122
Website: www.eyediscover.com

Library of Congress Control Number: 2020942423

ISBN 978-1-7911-3208-8 (hardcover)

Printed in Guangzhou, China
1 2 3 4 5 6 7 8 9 0 24 23 22 21 20

082020
102119

Project Coordinator: John Willis
Designer: Mandy Christiansen

AV2 acknowledges Getty Images, iStock, and Shutterstock as the primary image suppliers for this title.

EYEDISCOVER provides enriched content, optimized for tablet use, that supplements and complements this book. EYEDISCOVER books strive to create inspired learning and engage young minds in a total learning experience.

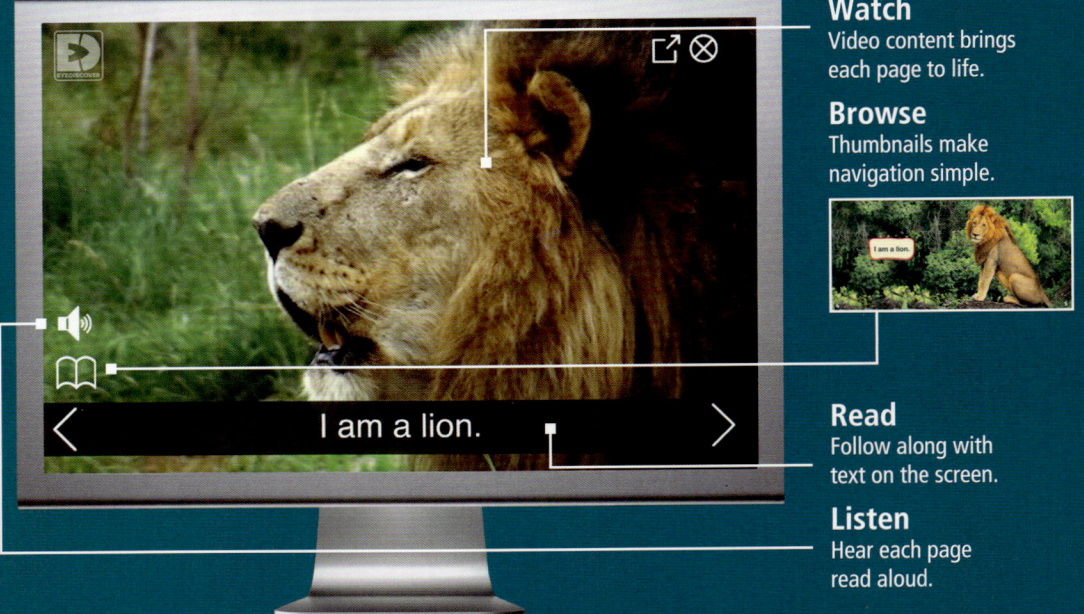

I am a lion.

Watch
Video content brings each page to life.

Browse
Thumbnails make navigation simple.

Read
Follow along with text on the screen.

Listen
Hear each page read aloud.

Your EYEDISCOVER Optic Readalongs come alive with...

Audio
Listen to the entire book read aloud.

Video
High resolution videos turn each spread into an optic readalong.

OPTIMIZED FOR

☑ **TABLETS**

☑ **WHITEBOARDS**

☑ **COMPUTERS**

☑ **AND MUCH MORE!**

Veterans Day

In this book, you will learn about

- what it is

- why people celebrate it

- how people celebrate it

and much more!

3

Veterans Day is celebrated in the United States on November 11 every year.

On Veterans Day, Americans honor everyone who has served in the U.S. military.

Veterans are celebrated for their heroism and patriotism.

Veterans Day was once called Armistice Day. It celebrated the end of World War I. Today, it celebrates all U.S. veterans.

11

People around the country celebrate Veterans Day with parades. The largest parade is in New York City.

13

A memorial service is held every Veterans Day at the Arlington National Cemetery in Virginia.

15

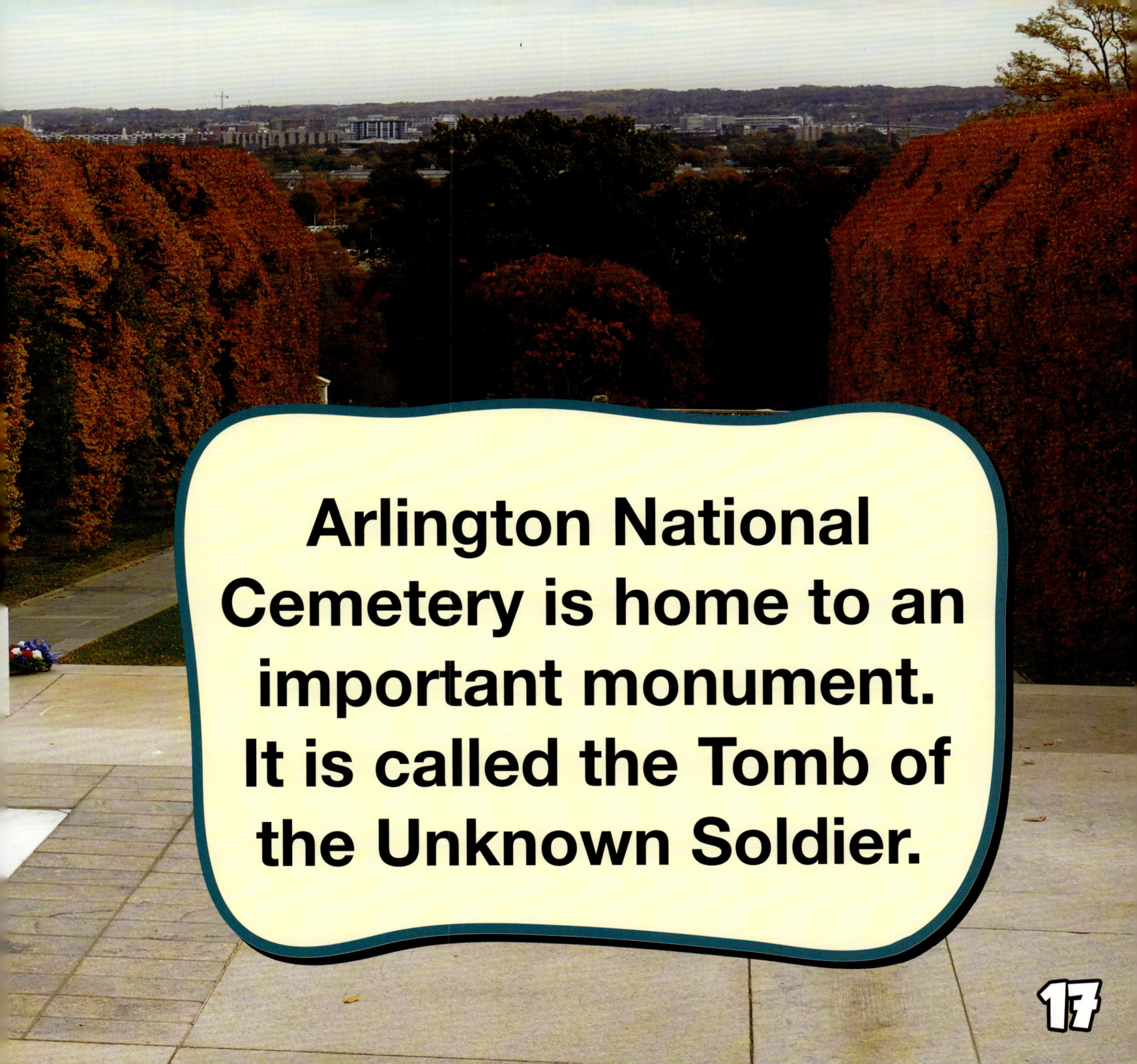

Arlington National Cemetery is home to an important monument. It is called the Tomb of the Unknown Soldier.

Another important memorial in Arlington is the Marine Corps War Memorial.

People display American flags on Veterans Day. This is a sign of support for the U.S. military.

VETERANS DAY BY THE NUMBERS

About 25,000 veterans come to the Veterans Day parade in **New York City** each year.

22

The United States has about **1.3 million** personnel on **active duty.**

The United States **military** has **six branches**.

Armistice Day became **Veterans Day** in 1954.

There are about **20.4 million veterans** in the United States.

23

KEY WORDS

Research has shown that as much as 65 percent of all written material published in English is made up of 300 words. These 300 words cannot be taught using pictures or learned by sounding them out. They must be recognized by sight. This book contains 36 common sight words to help young readers improve their reading fluency and comprehension. This book also teaches young readers several important content words, such as proper nouns. These words are paired with pictures to aid in learning and improve understanding.

Page	Sight Words First Appearance
5	day, every, in, is, on, states, the, year
6	Americans, has, who
9	and, are, for, their
10	all, end, it, of, once, was, world
13	around, city, country, new, people, with
14	a, at
17	an, home, important, to
18	another
21	this

Page	Content Words First Appearance
5	United States, Veterans Day
6	military
9	heroism, patriotism, veterans
10	Armistice Day, World War I
13	New York City, parades
14	Arlington National Cemetery, memorial service, Virginia
17	monument, Tomb of the Unknown Soldier
18	Marine Corps War Memorial
21	flags, sign, support

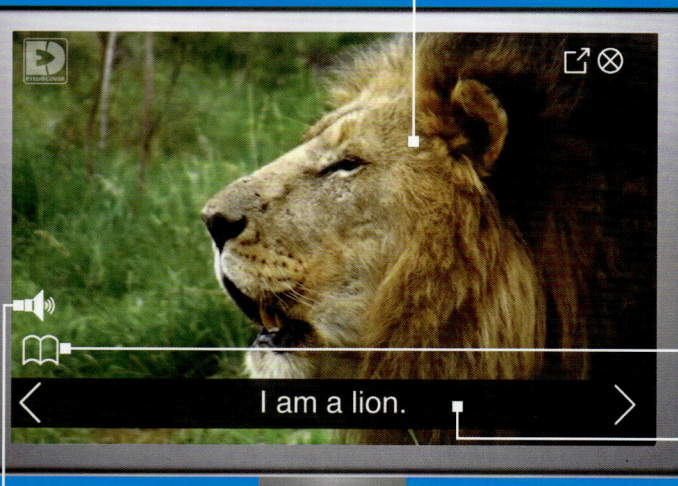

I am a lion.

Watch
Video content brings each page to life.

Browse
Thumbnails make navigation simple.

Read
Follow along with text on the screen.

Listen
Hear each page read aloud.

EYEDISCOVER

Go to **www.eyediscover.com** and enter this book's unique code.

BOOK CODE

AVL68349